How Sweet Must We Dream:
To Forget Such Troubling Nightmares

Desmond X Thompson

White Oak Edits

The Library of Congress has cataloged this record under LCCN 2025916641

ISBN (eBook): 979-8-9997294-1-5

ISBN (Paperback): 979-8-9997294-2-2

ISBN (Hardcover): 979-8-9997294-3-9

Contents

Skewed Brain

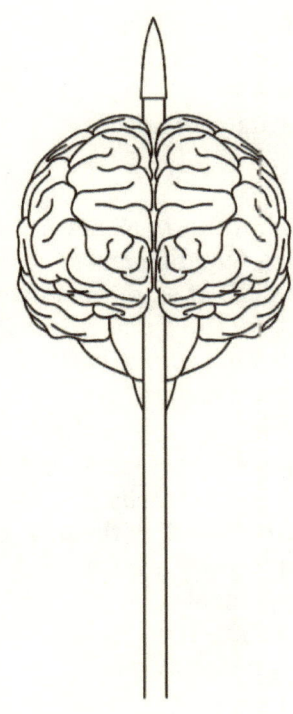

Touching Earth

A war on rogue emotion
Recovering from that first close loss
And now that you've figured it out
You don't know how to stop
Unsuccessfully convincing yourself
It's ok to be sad

The battle may be won but the work never ends
There is no choice but to schedule tears
Eyes are searching for signs of emotional plaque
Ears listen continuously to catch wavering syllables
If you can't be happy, stay in your room
That's probably what got you here

Migraines must be a side effect of torn intent
Trapped breath forcing its way through you
Not even air will bend to the will of the powerless
Polite suggestions do not move armies
The only thing you can control
Are tears from meeting soft earth
And everything else happens anyway

You Love Him (I'm Jealous)

He's smooth with a perfect shine
Polished by gods and spirits before placed on a pedestal
A modern minimalist statue
Even motionless he speaks volumes
A gem which brings bad luck only to me

I'm a rock in the bottom gravel of a stream
Incapable of hearing anything above the water's surface
The muffling current is but babbling internal noise
Rebuilding and destroying my own confidence
Rendering me unqualified to make choices

I grow ill at the thought of a version of me
Never tossed to deep achromatic liquid
Absorbing the sun's praise
Skipping effortlessly across crystal rivers
Passersby always find that perfect stone

A cold life in limbo with no stability or escape
I know his experience but only appreciate it once it's lost
A momentary frame of mind
Impossible to contain at paper's edge
If only he could chisel away that lesser half

Something Different

Would you call it poetry
Bleeding out in delirium
An unresponsive body thrown in the shower
The next day you made fun of me
Could you call that poetry

Would you call it poetry
Nagging you ask if I am free
Neglecting to atone for wrongful deeds
So many things that word could mean
Could you call that poetry

Would you call it poetry
Spirit ripping itself apart for that time which feels infinite
Blood boils when anyone wants to see or touch me
And I'd rather cry than be intimate
Could you call that poetry

What's Wrong

I digress once I start believing I need an exit strategy
No challenge can keep me from giving a requested smile
Should I speak plainly, I'd bite my tongue
Suffering in thought is a common experience after all
And everyone else is committing effortlessly

I deviate from bathrooms with cracked mirrors
A night out blurs the imperfections needing avoidance
Strangers beg for the deliberation of a new friendship
His scent of bourbon and sandalwood may be persuasive
Unfortunately that name would escape me on a sober day

I tend to believe something's wrong with me
I can't forget who I am, but I laugh when I speak
Troubling thoughts and wandering minds
Still, it'd be selfish to think of goodbyes

Catered to a Cause

The punchline of a subject in youth
Before even capable of knowing if it's true
The absurd rage from friends and family
For objecting to correct statements, said in a hurtful way
Simply because I couldn't know myself sooner

Finding new friends and even new family
Realizing what a community is, the solace entailed
Then whispers of the mind became embodied speakers
Maybe my dear blue fairy left before her job was done
In her defense, I thought vulnerability followed trust

I'm over the rainbow
I don't want an umbrella, I need a safety net
Who knew inclusion was capitalism, catered to a cause
I still lack money and abs so I guess I should give up
Objectify or abide by the standard way of things

Where is Home

Discovering this place can be distant and hardened
While searching everywhere for something never found
Aches and fractures are pitiful medals of exploration
In a world which never tells you what the grand prize is

The hills of Paradise seemed a mountainous trek
Branches became blindfolds instead of ladder rungs
Vines grow while trees rot and leave a fence-work of snags

Always lost and away from anything
But there is no home when all places bring a lonely chill
You can't trust a dishonest breeze
When sharp teeth still shine in the darkness

Stone Kingdom

A small rundown stone castle
Many kings and queens called it their home
Yet the owner of this haven stayed in shadows

A collective of people from all walks of life
Together under one roof
To celebrate any small achievement
Or share ideas and experiences
And of course, make new memories

The biggest tragedy was painting the stone wall
A new ruler without any love or care for old subjects
All hope was lost the second the music changed tune

Oklahoma

If I got a one-way ticket for tomorrow
Tell me, would I really be going home
My friends have friends
My family's half dead
So I usually end up alone
I know it's not dreamy here
My decisions aren't always too clear
Navigating night
Because you won't give me the day
You say you want me near
While you leave me in the darkness
I got this

Oklahoma never felt like home to me
The people may be nice
But they're cruel just as easily

My bones are shattered
My heart left a bruise
I'm going full speed to nowhere
What else could I do
Some dented pop can on the side of the street
I know I was born in winter
But crisp air makes me freeze
Reminds me I'm by myself
Even if people keep me in their thoughts

I appreciate the person it made me today
When we were corralled and stuck in one place
But that's the structure I hate

Accidental Serial Killer

I remember that experience parents say to cherish
The moment nobody knows about
The time you gave me an insightful opportunity
After an eternity away you came back into my life
And made it crumble as if the world fell from beneath me
Leaving me to live in the colorless void of space

It reminds me of the guy nobody ever brings up
He wanted me to burn because my existence was a burden
He failed and in a twist took his own life instead
What am I to assume if I'm not the criminal
Or some bad spirit sent to make people just give in

I regret not knowing how unhappy you were
The *married friends* story works in fairy tales and comedy
Am I some selfish accomplice for saying no
That guy had it coming
But you never should have gone

Old Best Friend

Old best friend
Where did we end
Did new toys break everything we built
No time for acknowledgments or apologies
Is your past a graveyard of forgotten oddities
Dear old best friend
I wish I could've seen the end

A sour apple once was sweet
So many changes you'll never see
I had to pick myself up in my darkest times
Were you smiling as he lied
Do you like the way he laughs as you cry
And the biggest joke of all is somehow me

Old best friend
Who had it best
In the end

Me & California

Never nice, always kind
I get migraines when I cry
No one cares about hollow smiles
Just act happy all the while

I had a bad day
Sorry to hear that
They don't ask if you're okay
Or even what happened

A flood of emotions
My expressions change constantly
Happy dolls in a happy place
They hate when it rains

Once beautifully blinded with romantics
I'd laugh at the mention of *peaceful* now
Quiet feuds burn soft light
Entertainment feeds the bored

The people around me are alive
I clash with California on subtle fronts
Don't we all just want to have fun
Surely happy isn't everyone's default

Lost in Translation

Maybe I should get some help
Hit up a counselor, or sit in my room like it's a cell
I ponder life and the notion I could change
It must be normal, grinning through all this pain
Watching glass for hours and burning through clouds
What do you have to show for it

Is he cute, or am I bored
Life is nothing but pointless chores
Drinking bottles just for the sport
So few moments, so many people to ignore

Maybe I should get to class
Hit up the gym, or sit on my lazy ass
I wonder if I could ever fly
Would I soar through the air
Or lay staring at the sky

Should this be fun, or am I just sad
Doomed to be a failure
Just like my dad

Is he lame, or am I behind
Life is nothing but wasted time
Drinking bottles just for the sport
So few moments, so many people to ignore
So many people

Scarce

I don't want to reclaim my youth
I'm trying to find that joyful spirit
I used to be...

Liars cheats and thieves run a society
I once believed was free
I would have never guessed
One day nature herself would be called fake
I dare not wonder why she is angry

We could change the world
Well, we are, but not in the ways I'd planned
I grew up thinking people had power
It's disheartening to know corporations do
How is a small-town nobody
Supposed to overthrow billion-dollar superpowers
It's medieval villagers
Versus giant robots

How can any adult have a joyful spirit
In a society where you're either sad and suppressed
Or constantly angry about anything others do
Even if they don't negatively affect anyone
Such intricate distractions
To keep rich men operating their robots
And poor people fighting for bread
While, all the while, not acknowledging
Food is scarce

Broken Bone

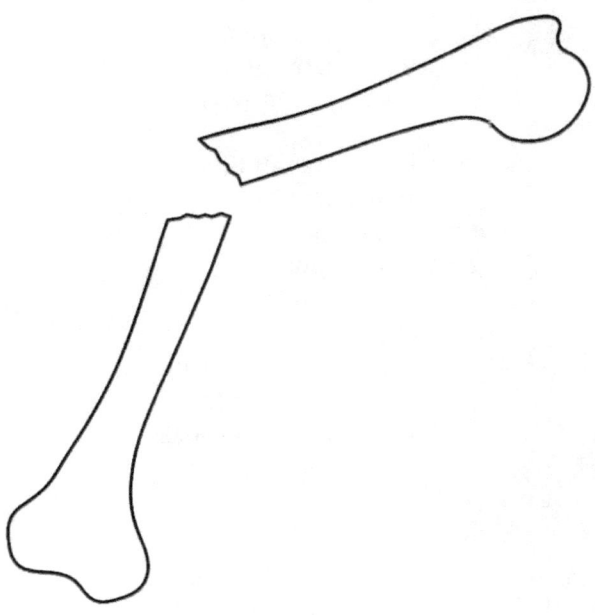

Better Tomorrow

A busy bee
Has no time to flee
But dreams about
Flying seven seas

Leaving the vomit filled air
A true life lived, without any care
Not looking back, at what is away
Sleeping on poppies all day

A busy bee
And good fantasy
Tries not to pout
While feeling the breeze

Dream Forest

Even alone I will survive
A mosaic enduring floods fires drought and snow
Perseverance
Constantly searched for and never seen
But here I stand

Always in between
My envy evergreen
Small fires grow
Obscene
A crowded canopy
Shadows choking
Everything growing below

Explore my meadows, they're melancholy
But the streams are pure of doubt
That once riddled my beloved body
Something which yearns acknowledgment
But is still scared of being destroyed

I don't want to be a dream forest
A dream forest
A dream

The Quest of Purpose

Riding down the river
Running through the plains
Screaming in the canyon
Like we have gone insane
Diving in the ocean
Dancing through the rain
I know somewhere we can go
Find me where you are

Singing to bats as they sleep
Making snake statues in the snow
Reading into every conspiracy
Trucking with the highs and the lows
Talking in the tall Red Woods
Taking any chance we get
I know somewhere we can go
Just find me where you are

Nature's Looking Glass

My friends laugh and tease each other safe on the shore
I let them know I need a moment longer
Away from the warm fire and deeper into the lake's wonderful
        darkness

A moonless sky gives the stars freedom to be admired
I surrender my body to the still water
My head and feet travel in opposing unison
Fusing two realities together
Chatty friends can no longer be heard
There is only the pulsing of my chest and the ripples running
        across the surface
Navy silhouettes of trees carry little attention as I lay in nature's
        mirror
The stars gaze upon the dense oak forest and its elongated
        looking glass

A dancing fire entertains small creatures while one lies alone
As if a bug on the windshield of a car
The cosmic rarity reflecting the stars themselves
Holding the creature in time
Suspended in space and unburdened by the world around him
Blacks blues and twinkling white lights
For a moment all possible existences merge
An unfathomable occurrence
Witnessed by one tiny creature wishing to be alone

Brilliant Beauty

It's weird
The pleasantries of the forest
How the hills dance along the horizon
Brushing the setting sun

Yet in the city
Tall buildings block the sunset views
With loud noises silencing all peace
Still they bring clever minds together

And in the mountains
If you're not on top
The giant beasts stretch over the sun
Bringing the day to an early close

Even on the beach
Every gorgeous sunset is on a quickened timer
A brilliant beauty
Quickly lost

Precious Choices

Fool's gold
Even I was dumb enough to look at it
Dead in the eyes
And call it something valuable

Diamonds
Every one comes with some flaw
Even if it's not physical
But everybody is smitten with them

Garnet
A resplendent gem
A diversity of under-appreciated colors
Yet as random to say
Perfect

For the Unseen Audience

I would rather be alone
Than encourage neglecting my spirit
Having a say in my solitude is comfort enough

Carefully crafting plans
Like a well-made fabric
A gorgeous structure
But highly flammable

I would rather talk to myself
Than have my words fall on deaf ears
Meaningful conversation rarely has an audience

Beautifully heartfelt lyrics
Such well-intended purpose
Sitting in a veil of dust
While listeners tour an endless library

They Danced

I saw the future
And it was pretty boring
Clouds blew over
And the rain from above began to pour
Late in the night
There wasn't a light to be seen
The animals danced and sang
Giving life a whole new meaning
What is there to learn from the mistakes
We always make
What can we do when so many things
Are constantly changing

I saw the future
And it was pretty boring
The sun began to rise
The rain stopped its pouring
The remnants of youth now covered up
In a tired green
The animals paused to watch
Wondering what I must be thinking
There's beauty in the silence
My friends usually fill with words
But even the usual can be irregular
And not all songs can be heard
How do you help or know when you should
I ponder solutions for what is the greater good

The Violent Things

A harmless pearlescent bubble
Blowing through a windstorm
It could have broken and still may break
From the moment it was brought into existence

The maze of thorns grow in resistance
A noted threat surrounding this carefree child
Spectators shout a mix of encouragement and critiques
The future holds complete success or expected failure

Fickle little sphere
Always needing guidance
Keeping the masses in wait
A life televised without request

Flying Opossum

Citrus pinks and tired purples saturate a blushing sky
Warm air meets cold north winds
Maple trees giggle in the passing breeze
Tall grasses and forbs play tag just outside of the forest
Distant city lights multiply with every dimming moment
Amusing spectacles of routine activities
What dangers are in the dark
When dangers cannot reach you

Striking oranges and jealous blues seek attention notably
Scarce beams of light shoot through the horizon
Birds ready for their nightly travels
Brooding clouds make their way to familiar places as well
Creatures are eager for bed or a late-night breakfast
Such strange wonders are seen from above
What use have you for playing dead
When you can fly

Nightmare

The pack swarms a merlot-stained figure
Towering glass walls offer little shelter
Monstrous creatures of comparable size barrel through
Like air filling a narrow cavity
The figure falls to a once beautiful rug
A simple object that had previously been unacknowledged
For the subtle comfort and power to calm that it possessed
Now a mess of crimson and earth
The fallen victim can no longer run but crawls
A desperate attempt to change its fate
The rug offers one last moment of peace
As the thing clings tightly to it before going still
In anticipation of what could never change

After This

It must be real
That beautiful place I have seen before
The warm intense light that should leave me wincing
Embracing cool shadows
And a breeze always passing by
At just the right speed

A kaleidoscope of colors
Sparkling reflections on pristine water flow by
Crossing rocks and guiding gorgeous animals
All at peace and cooperating instinctively

A vast forest and endless beach yet nobody feels forgotten
Everyone contributing to this utopic state of existence

Frozen Water

Winter snow
The last of the year
The first of the year
Ain't that just the way

A hoard of snowflakes
Sacrificing their form
An attempt to make warmth cold
Biting at the fingertips

An avalanche
The massive army enraged
Claiming a domination victory
Staying close to those they love

Take What You Have

A star dies
In a galaxy far away
Such a shame
It was already gone before anyone could see
Nobody noticed
The spectacular and riveting light

What if all we had
Was good enough to want to stay
What if moving on
Was not an option or a choice
We would ever have to make

Do we think too much
And enjoy too little
Everything burns out so quickly
And the weight of this life lingers

Is a new horizon just that of yesterday
Only viewed in new apparel
Maybe we can't stomach the chaos we create

A star dies
Before we can even see it
What joys and wonders were there
In that place we will never know is gone

The Quantum Theory of Everything

Time, it flows like a river
But only to the physical plane
Which must abide by its pressure
A linear path to us, a celestial mist to the spirit world

Surely time's dominion over us is only equal
As our influence over the spirit world
Where which you control your destiny
We are responsible for the afterlife we are assigned
Where do you genuinely believe you deserve to be

Spirits of course, are not confined to a single place in time
The afterlife could be infinite
A constant beauty of all you adore and cherish
Or an endless lesson never learned
But you may go in time itself, and let your soul be reborn
Because naturally, all mist will eventually be part of a river

Flash Beetles

A city of moving lights
A colony of high-spirited creatures
Providing free light for all
And harming none
Yet most call them flies with fire
Undermining their brilliance
Dismissive of their talents

A regal body of golds, reds, and blacks
Bioluminescence flashing yellowish green
A bold statement, possibly the boldest ever
Displayed by a nocturnal creature

A traveling art show
A civilization of eager love bugs
Late-night callers
Photogenic stars
Of the forests, plains, and swamps
Not a firefly
A flashing beetle

Be Calm Sweet Pet

The impatient waters of a restless river
Flooding shades glimmer in blue
Drowning out desperate noise

A shimmering canvas glistening wet
The most stunning view from above
A reckless beast keeping shapes hidden below

Fleeing bubbles of air abandon their creator
An act of pure self-preservation instinctively
The freezing liquid cradles warm tears

Be calm sweet pet

Carved Heart

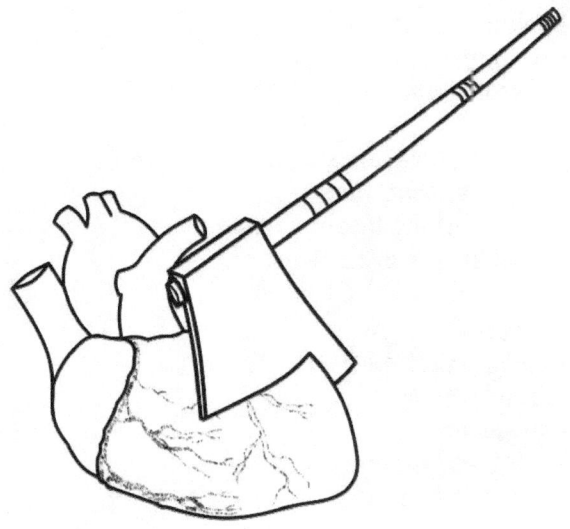

Seasons of Love

Dance parties when we're all alone
Sweet sweet nothings on the phone
Now I'm stuck in this quiet room
Why did you leave
I want to wake up in your bed
But still you're in my head instead
Why do our bodies make such callous dreams

Thought that I could love you through the summer
Winter days are ones that make you older
Maybe we had something but now it's over
Hearts that fall in spring are always colder

It's crazy how I think of you
As if this time had never flew
Not trying to sound bitter
But isn't life so sweet
Playing through these memories of joy
Didn't know I was always your toy
Better to see it now than never I suppose

Thought that I could love you through the summer
Winter days are ones that make you older
Maybe we had something but now it's over
Hearts that fall in spring are always colder

Blind

I don't want to fall, I want to float
Like a cloud being blown away
By your devotion

Impress me and I'll get it
Empress, me? I hardly feel it
But you try

If doves cry and swans sing
What could you call a frog's noise
I'd like a chorus

I don't give up, I give my all
Will he read this or let words fade
They lie in wait

Did we go back to where we were
As if I never heard any hateful things
Am I blind

Happy Meds

I'm just smoking on a ciggy
Hun it ain't no biggie
Cancer kills you slow
But time will kill you faster
The clock is always spinning
While I'm waiting for your call
I should run away
But you know I'd only fall

You're heartbreak in a bottle
A poison in my veins
If I had you in my life
I'd never be the same

You're so charming
You're brilliant, and beautiful
I can't meet up to those standards
When I'm always feeling miserable
Potential pain, this price I pay
With you I can see better days

You're a legend and an artist
A sunrise I will not soon forget
If this pill gets too hard to swallow
I'll still choke on it

Artifacts

You can't trust such rogue impulses
Ideas of entangled dreams
You act like this is an easy game
However delicate spirits are nothing to win
You can't speak of forever after
As if the story stops being told
You may say I'm your beacon of life and energy
Time is best at changing everything

Love is something simple
But a thing too difficult to escape
It leaves you lost in its blindness
Just so you can't get away
It has you wondering
Could there be any better days
A reluctant breath during an extended vacation
You're biting your lip, wishing it will last forever

Who knew love could be an artifact
Something real, yet so unknown
Who has conceived it to be so fragile
Though it leaves you filled with broken bones
Who thought it tasted absurdly bitter
Like someone left out the good tea
Who said at the end of it all, was nothing but alone
A self-fulfilled calamity

Why

I'd be your new toy, if it meant charging by your side
On the nightstand or left in the living room
I don't care, as long as I'm on your mind
Do you not realize
My service *disintegrates* without you near

I'd hit rewind
If it meant I could stay a blank screen
Before the day you turned me on
The hour my logic board caught fire
There's no repairing the damage you caused
By simply letting me know you exist
I wish I could hate you

I'd be happy too
If my mind never suffered such perplexity
Being able to delete the person I called friend
Shrugging off those three words that changed everything
Such flattery, but things were easier
Just searching for compliments
You must be so relieved I'm gone

Torment

Again you avoid my gaze
A stranger who happens to be at the same table
Distraction demands absolute attention
What beauty is there in a painting
When you've seen it a hundred times over
Baroque is *hopeless* compared to Art Nouveau in her prime

Spotlights shift and even recent compliments seem ancient
Am I to be placed in storage once the dust hides my gloom
Not even a lavish frame could keep you focused on me
When there's joyous vibrant roses to cheer you up
Instead of bleak hues constantly needing enlivened
A dark blue is no match for any bright seductive color

When fantasy burns a hole in you
Should it be appreciated for its appeal and efforts
Though they rid you obsolete and dated
Meet my eyes even if for one small moment
I'll rejoice at the idea you see my value beneath this veil
How do you so effortlessly torment me

Goodbye

Hold-on to the longing in my eyes
When you say you have to go this time
I pushed my palm against that warm chest
Yet you grabbed my wrist to pull me closer
One hand free to run fingers across your cheek
While you studied my soft and aspiring lips
Before I leaned in you met me for a kiss
Say that you won't but I know you will
You'll miss me when I'm gone

The Rift

Don't miss that story too much
I fell short of catching the perfect ending
Times always seem so different
When I'm standing next to you

Chemistry and stardust
Could never fix the hole between us
The rift it grew and split our paths in two

It was perfect for a moment
Adventures kept us going
You'd hold me close
And all our troubles would fade away

It was some epic romance
But time always creates distance
And from this point
I see nothing we can do

I know I'll always be
Your favorite shade of blue
But I don't love you

Venture Past

I think of you now, and there's only a tired heavy old fabric
At one time I found comfort holding you over me
Like a weighted blanket
Practically breathless and unable to see what's past you
A movie played a story I could faintly hear
But I should have already known it well
We couldn't stay together because we lost the plot
You'd caress every inch of me as I absorbed your cold

We aspired for a future grounded in mutual understanding
No, I must have been the one existing without living
A fabric used to shield never holds such complex thoughts
Blankets don't belong in dreams, they only help you sleep
When tears abandon my eyes, the pillow catches them
High expectations of simple things indeed

As the chime of a song I once loved signals the movie's end
What am I to do but mourn a once comfortable pastime
A lifeless sheet, a dull ponderous blanket
And a pillow full of secrets

"Forget About It"

Every atom of oxygen being heaved from your body
The fragrance of late spring
A stubborn man who thinks he's right
Is this what peace should sound like

A kindness for someone who can't return the favor
The hidden resentment you feel too stupid to bring up
That kiss before an overdue goodnight
Why do we think things are alright

Traveling the world in search of far-off places
Locking yourself in your room
Experiencing the vastness of creation's light
What times can we not forgive tonight

Infatuation

I have no right to think about you
Yet I can't seem to make myself stop
Drinking myself into a puddle
Maybe then you'll pick me up
At least I'll feel half as good
As I did with you near me
I only want to breathe your air
Even if it's just infatuation
Please let me live out the fantasy

I could ruin your life
Then help you put it back together
Let me be the navigator who drives you mad
With ropes at the ready to tie you up until you feel better
Our interests in line to an absurd degree
You badger me with empty propositions
Yet your hands drift onto me so consistently
One day I will hold you in suspense
Begging as you enjoy making me do

Empty

I wish I could care for you
But my mind has twisted to a distorted form
I hold you in my dreams
Only to remember I can't want you

All the wicked things about me
Are ripping through this gentle shell
A cicada pulling from the hollow nymph
Time has changed me

Stare me down with those sad eyes
Maybe soon I'll forget to breathe
All this longing
Makes me empty

Grow Up

Loving you makes muscles soft and eyes weary
The disappointment I endured dulled all senses
According to you, we were stuck like glue
More like a car broke down in the rain

Without your shadow blocking the sun, I can feel
As if above the graveyard, I am alive again
Fear of judgment has turned into a desire for experience
Not even the light of the moon can push me to bed

I am sound when I sleep
Awake for the day with no hesitation
My daydreams are vivid and inspiring
The rain gives me hope something new may grow

Good times depend on more than seasons
Hardships are holes in an ever-winding road
I am that of a seed in fertile soil
Something beautiful which requires time

Self-hatred

Sorry to make you dizzy
By the choices of my clothes
They say trailblaze, but I'm bulldozing

Objectification is a motive
Shooting down everyone
And calling it ambition

You could be my new distraction
Hold me under sheets or under waves
Your kiss was more than I had imagined

Drowning in tears with a perfect view
You yearn for even a brief touch
When I am but a frigid figure in the distance

Apologies I caused a stir
You say I broke your heart
Yes I heard, but that memory evades me

It's a strange yet special type of self-hatred
I would cross oceans
When you don't want me

The Good Guy

Thought you'd always love kissing me
Turns out I'm nothing but poison
Your arrogance claimed I'd forever want you back
But that dynamic seems revolting
So you run back to your ex
Turns out I'm the one he's been calling
Fake men keep saying I'm bad news
But my reputation keeps soaring

I'm a good guy
They say don't judge a book by its cover
I guess that's why
Wicked people make such good lovers
I'm a good guy
Well, that's what you said
Don't blame me

I am disappointed
You thought of me as a badly written character
Confident in judging me
Yet you were nothing but wrong
A truly bleak mind playing a clever evil
I bet you'd apologize if you knew I caught on

Songbird

How could anyone love a songbird
They always sing when they aren't told
Constantly the same few notes

How could you ever love a songbird
When all they like is to hear themselves sing
You'd think that sound would get old

To me you're just a bird
Always looking for anyone's attention
Something that chirps but is never heard
How could I ever love a songbird

Prolonged Realization

My eyes are open
But my body won't move
Frozen by a numbing truth
A rage stirs as acceptance whispers
This life destroyer is trying to sell me another touch
A worried smile and extended hand
Those eyes were never sad
They simply try desperately to fill a void

I could not possibly believe my affection alone was enough
I sacrificed daily for the vortex trying to be whole
As months flew the subtle requests became loud demands
Today I'm beautiful, yesterday I was useless
All those promises, none of that was ever true
Hollow creatures are only interested in the short-term
We're friends, just friends, *always* friends
But hold me, kiss me, tell me I'm attractive

I see through the damaged beast
Pinning me down with a soft smile and rough hands
I don't have the magic to break this hex
Or was the curse playing with monsters to begin with
I don't even think I ever really loved you for you

Mr. Charming

Even when you're hurting me
Your voice is unbearably charming
We pass under the lights of the theme park
Wondering when our dreams won't be so disheartening
And on the most recent day you left
The candle in my chest went out
A numb neutrality which serves no purpose
But don't worry, I'll be fine

I know you've erased me
To find someone simple, with a consistent glow
Less maintenance and trauma
A puppet with no backstory
I'll read the warning label out loud next time
Though an honest exit implies a closed door

What a nauseating ride
We return to the same artificial stars every weekend
I can't be happy knowing my amusements aren't enough
I haven't felt pain, quite like this
Even when you're hurting me
Your voice is so unbearably charming

Never Again

One second
I'm supposed to be here with friends
You've paid such close attention to me though
My stories hardly ever hold people in suspense
Perhaps I could stay for that last drink

One second
Even draping my legs across you on the couch
You seem like you're existing on a different plane
A gentle kiss on my wrist assures me you've returned
And I might forget the possibility tomorrow is never-after

One second
You're a road trip to nowhere
But I enjoy seeing you drive shirtless through the hills
Hot like the inside of this car in the middle of summer
Maybe I will let my mind take the back seat

One second
And just like that
It's like it never happened

Plastic Doll/Bleeding Heart

You only love me for my brain
When I take off my clothes I'm a supermodel
If I'm on my knees for you
I'm a statuesque entity striking a pose
You like that I'm so exceptionally open minded
When there's experiments you want to attempt
You say you want to get to know me
But at what point have you tried

My body may be art to you, but you're a piece of work
You know what to say, though you rarely mean it
And you ruined my new shirt
I'm a loveless loser who has passion pulsing in my veins
Playing house was fun, but don't pretend that I'm okay

I only love you for the notion
We may be enamored with one another someday
Thought if we spent time together long enough
These emotions would make me feel more sane
I'm a plastic doll with a bleeding heart
Tired of laying down
Does any man make any plan past sunset until dawn
Forever waiting for that one
Not lying just for fun

Colder are October Days

Colder are October days
The ones I'm scared to enjoy
Good times remind me when we'd have fun
My laugh and your awful noise
You pushed me away
As if a car was coming straight for me
The hero act was always your suit
But these days I'm avoiding all saviors

You give nothing but bad stories
Fairy tales
That I find really boring
Turns out I don't even need you
Why have a man that weighs me down
When I can enjoy the breeze of open skies

If you're looking for a hand to hold
Mine are not for you
Act like we'd have a future
But the lies of man are nothing new
You used to look into my eyes
With forever longing
Now I feel lobotomized in June
Cracked my heart and ran away
I guess damaged goods won't do
Play the good guy all you want
I get it (fuck you)

Breaking Teeth

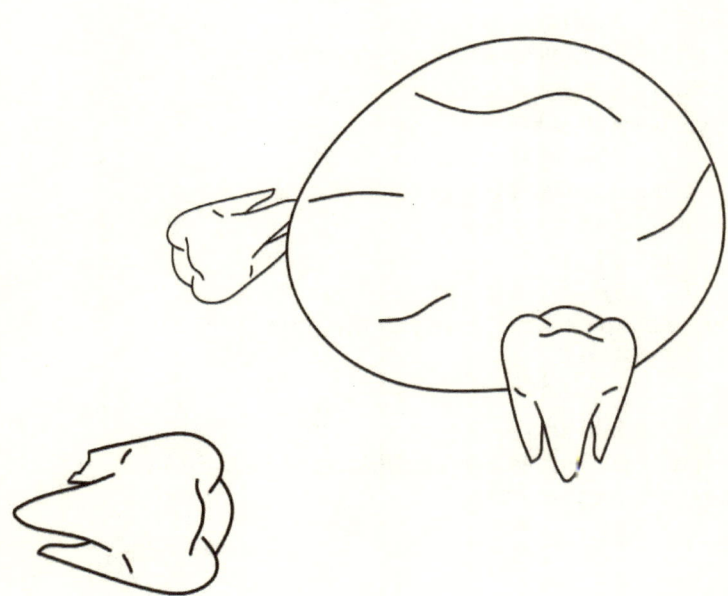

There is no Mars

I'm watching stars and you're chasing planets
Have fun Mr. Astronaut
That's not butterflies upsetting my stomach
Your pickup lines are cheesy
And I'm lactose intolerant

Life's sole purpose isn't finding a soulmate
Sadness just longs for a warm fire
What's your sign
Damaged
But people shop at thrift stores all the time

Look at me
Right on schedule and in the lines
Who knew work before work could feel so rewarding
They say my Mars is in Virgo

Marble Man

I need a man (made of marble)
10 foot if he stands
But he don't bother
Got abs, like, damn
But no one want em
Those lips could hurt me
If they lied
But they ain't gonna
I need a marble man

Maybe Medusa had it right
Cause statues never leave
He'd always be here for me
And listen when I speak
He never snaps back, or argues
I'd never worry, like I do
Always waiting for me
So quiet and patiently

I need a man (made of marble)
10 foot if he stands
But he don't bother
Got abs, like, damn
But no one want em
Those lips could hurt me
If they lied
But they ain't gonna
I need a marble man

Sweet Babes

I wanna watch you while you sleep
I won't make a peep
I swear
The hold you have on me
You're something so unique
Hi there
Watching you's better than counting sheep
I won't make a peep
I wanna watch you while you sleep

What We Can

It's just like death eating a cracker
Before she downs a lemon sour
Doing what we can
But we only get paid by the hour

And wow
What a trip
Wish we had time to fill
Hoping to just live life
Instead of always trying to survive

It must be death eating a cracker
Before she downs a lemon sour
Doing what we can
But we only get paid by the hour

And wow
Ain't it swell
This cozy place we all call hell
I mean it's pretty hot
But being cool is just an after thought

I feel like death eating a cracker
Before she downs a lemon sour
Doing what we can
But we only get paid by the hour

Self-esteem

If I'm alone in the world at the end of the day
I know, I still have me
Why do I need someone when truth is
Alone is how I stay free
Heartbreak is a love mistake
You need yourself to fill the time
Overdo, is an I love you
Sorry boys but this is goodbye

What use is a heart of gold
When they never look past your face
What's the reason in being good
When they only care what's below the waist
What's the point in falling in love
If you're only going to be replaced
I don't get it
So I won't pretend

If I'm alone in the world at the end of the day
I know, I still have me
Self-care is a love affair
That could never end with some tragedy
Take your time but I won't waste mine
Acting as if you're some prince to be
Use the mirror if you need compliments
I'm not here for your self-esteem

Piercing Lungs

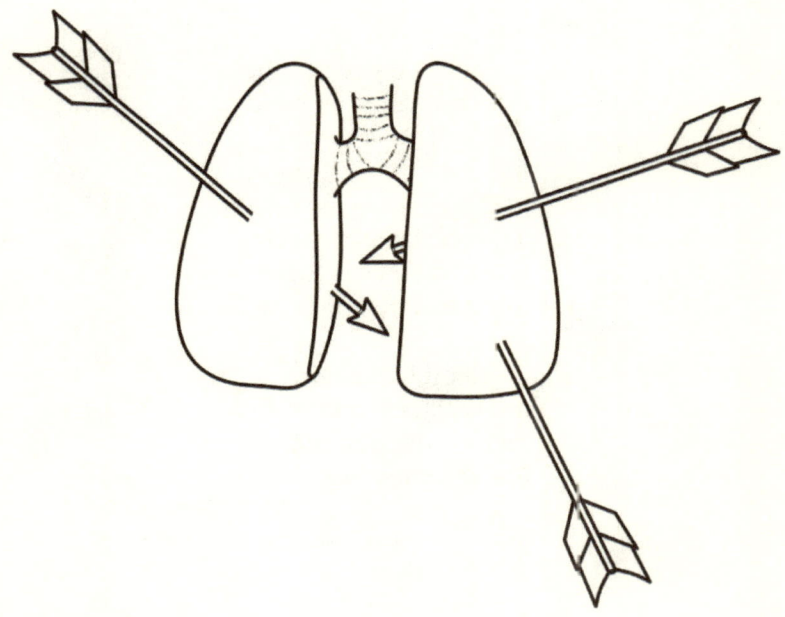

Castles & Fools

I'll give you a book
And I'll give you a stone
One will bring you peace
The other a throne

The burning pages
Of your favorite book
What history is there
If you can't hear it or look

Let it be known
You will have no throne
Your castles abandoned
You're family disowned

Like Glass

The Goddess of my life
The protector of my heart
How can the moon only have 8 phases
You wear so many hats, and in a variety of states
You are the reason I stay together

Strong enough to fight an army all on her own
Smart enough to answer any question
How could I ever grow to be that perfect
You taught me the importance of independence

Be careful, glass is fragile.
That means if you're not gentle, you'll hurt it,
And it will be hard to fix after that.
Oh, people are like glass too, right?
I wish more people thought so.

Devotion

I once believed leverage to be the most powerful force
Now I know that not to be true
Truly the most powerful force on earth is devotion
A slippery eel, difficult to obtain
And even harder still to keep in your grasp

So many people attach a great deal of words
To the meaning of love
Love is one word with one profound meaning
A word constantly being chained to others
As if they hold no power on their own
I love you, I care for you deeply
Other emotions often result from love
But those are things to be identified specifically
Love's numerous side effects
Should never be simplified or dumbed down

I admire the way you push through all hardships
I respect the mentation you put behind all your decisions
I appreciate that you care for others in a way I see few do
I support you and all of your ventures
I am devoted to you

Manipulating

Appreciation is shown, not said
Try harder if you want me to believe
You adore me so much you forget to say it

I care
I care when you act
I care when you act like the victim
I care when you act like the victim, and I'm the fool
I care when you act like the victim, and I'm the fool who
        never tries

Consideration has intention, not neglect
If I am truly that naive
I hope only to perish quickly

I don't care
I don't care to be manipulated
I don't care to be manipulated by anyone
I don't care to be manipulated by anyone who doesn't care
I don't care to be manipulated by anyone who doesn't care
        for me

S.F.S.

Mama, please don't blame me for what I've done
You know of all your kids
I've had it worse than anyone

I'm a fuck up but you still love me
I guess even a broken record has its use
At least I didn't abandon the family

I'll leave this world to no one else
I'd rather spend money on you and Mim
Than raise a child in this hell

Mama, I'm so fucking sorry
Maybe if I had kids or a husband with a picket fence
You'd find the time to stand up for me

Family Meeting

Gutted because I never stay
Yet oblivious to how miserable I was there
What would be different
Going back to the same old
To live a same old existence

I have two bad spirits on both my shoulders
The one thing *you* never do is apologize
And the one thing *you* never do is mean it
But I'm always the one making bad decisions

An intervention because of me
Oh, I mean it should be flattering
Usually I'm the one being ignored
That is unless of course, I can be of service
Then again, it's always forgotten

Two bad spirits
The one thing I know *you'll* always do
Is blame everyone for your own lack of effort
And the one thing I know *you'll* always do
Is put us back in the toy box
When you're done playing house

Invincible Villain

It must feel good
Being so untouchable
So blissfully unaware
You're more trouble than you're worth

I'm sure it feels nice
Never being called a fuck up
Even though you never sacrifice
You just take it all for granted
Everything you get
That you didn't earn

Are you the world's worst hero
Or just a villain
The superpower to make everyone forget
Every bad deed or insult
In an instant

I'm well aware
These are the unpleasant facts
You may not murder
But your presence turned my heart to ash
I always suspected I'd be made the bad guy

Heart, Mind, & Bones

But you think Arkansas is free
You love that fantasy more than me
No amount of kindness that I bring
Can thaw your heart
Not even after spring
You think Arkansas is free

You think Arkansas is free
Do you know how impossible that would be
No, all this healing can't numb the sting
It blows my mind
Dealt with this my whole life
But you think Arkansas is free

But you think Arkansas is free
Never believe in me
My accomplishments will never mean a thing
Dust and bones
One of only two people always there
You think Arkansas is free

White Cat

Some may have called you a stray
They were fools
You were always family to us
An outspoken beauty
A true hero in disguise

Nobody could know you and not love you
Everybody knows that smile
You were an inspiration to be brave
An overzealous dreamer
A woman with little opportunity

I will always love you
Everyone can attest
You weren't perfect, but a perfect teacher
An amazing role model
A badass with a white cat

Dear Papa

I called you on your birthday
Usually, I surprise you with a visit
What a cruel gift
Now that I didn't get to follow through
On a traditional I myself invented years ago

I feel awful
I miss you
I love you

You're not known for being kind
Or subtle by any means
You're the funny one
The man of few words and many jokes
I love your jokes
And when it counts, like, really *really* counts
You do give great advice
And always make me feel so much stronger
Capable of facing any hardship

I'm sorry I wasn't there
I'm sorry I made you cry
I love you

I Love You Most

You ask me what's wrong
Such a simple question shouldn't bring me to tears
Why is it now I can't hold them back

A decision must be made
Do I tell you something that will shatter your world
Though ignorance is bliss

The quality of one's life must be weighed
I never cared to be remembered
Until you started to forget

My heart hammers against my chest
As if trying to escape the unbearable rattlings of my mind
How sweet must we dream
To forget such troubling nightmares

Giving Blood

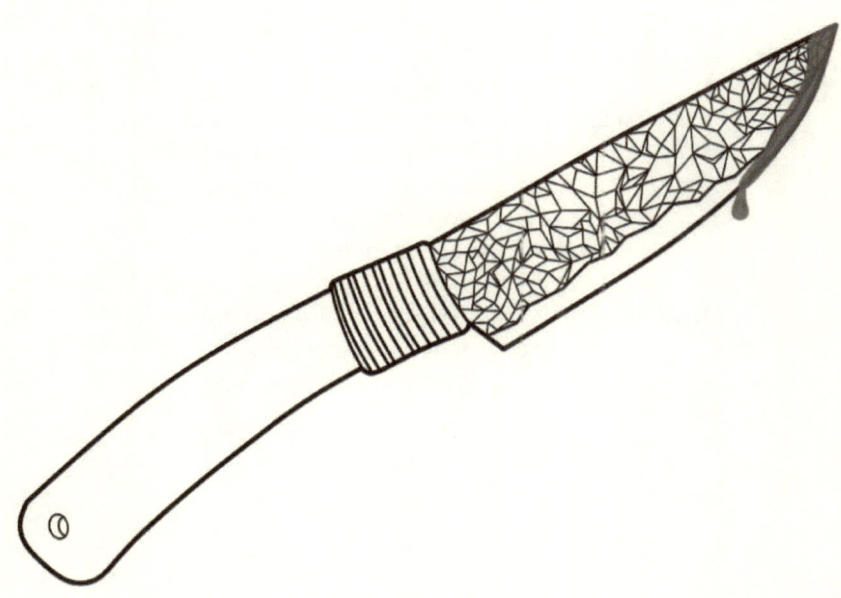

Letter From the Magic Mirror

If only you spent more time trying
to sincerely enjoy what you can make
of this world with the people who care
for you, and spend less time trying
to pretend you're some amazing
always happy person without any
limits or fears of criticisms from others.
Just imagine what a truly epic life you could live.
I wish you every happiness.
One day, I hope you wish the same.

Reasoning

There's an unrealized reassurance in not having dreams
Waking with a blank slate and only yesterdays' fumbles
Avoiding the captivation of seeing the life of a better you
The worthy individual feeling moths dancing in his chest

With superpowers you can break through walls
The average must find ways around before going forward
This world is too rigid for shortcuts and flair
A slow-paced series rather than two hours in cinema

Developed characters are made with a story set to unfold
Maybe that's why dreams have meaning
Was I born without a defined purpose
Or am I just a developing character

Spineless

It's hard to treat people as if they have braincells
When all they've shown is brain-rot
Since when do zombies have good table manners

Officially they would watch their neighbors starve
Rather than take the role of Big Brother
Too scared to fight or too selfish to stand

Lifeless creatures accusing others of treating them unfairly
But they'd rather eat their neighbor
Than acknowledge their unjust deeds

Trailer Park Queen

Run away now
Trailer Park Queen
To glitz and glam
And places serene
Planted things stay
And waste their lives away
So run away now
Trailer Park Queen

Run away now
Trailer Park Queen
From those chickens you loved
And those boys who were mean
Your grandma will miss you
And you will need a tissue
But run away now
Trailer Park Queen

Run away now
Trailer Park Queen
If life keeps feeling heavy
And you're sick of being knocked off your feet
It's your turn to choose
And what have you to lose
Run away
Trailer Park Queen

Well Aware

Beauty is not pain-inducing
It's embracing
The joyous experience of knowing
You feel as beautiful and expressive on the inside
As you look and behave on the outside

I'm not toxic
I'm corrosive
If you think you don't deserve me
You're right

I don't want somebody who makes me lose my words
Or my breath
I want someone who makes me feel comfortable
And capable of being loved
I'm more than stardust
I am cosmic existence

For a New Mom

Encouraging Thoughts & Sketches from a
Former New Mother to You

SUZANNE WYLDE

For you, a new mother.

I see you and all that you're doing and going through.

You are a wonderful mom.

CONTENTS

DISCLAIMER AND NOTE ON MY WRITING

I am not a therapist or a specialist in postpartum issues.
Please seek medical and/or psychiatric help if you need
it for any reason, including postpartum depression or
anxiety. My writing is not intended to replace medical
advice or therapy. Also, there are a ton of resources out
there, but I haven't listed them because they vary so
much between countries and states, but do seek out
support in your area if you need it.

I also want you to know that I wrote this from my
point of view mainly as a mother who was pregnant
and breastfed for a bit – I know that isn't everybody's
experience. While I don't want to exclude anyone, I felt
I had to write what I knew. To all the other mothers,
you are amazing moms too.

I attempt humor in places, so please don't take my
writing too literally. Also, I am a British woman living
in the States, so some of you may get thrown by my
accent (if listening to the audiobook) and others may

wonder why I use words like "mom" and "diaper". That's why, but I hope you can still relate to my words and the meaning behind them.

Finally, a small note about my use of AI. I don't use AI to write, I write the old-fashioned way. However, I do use it to tell me that I have put all the commas in the wrong, places. I don't use it to generate anything, however, so for better or worse what you're about to read is all me!

INTRODUCTION

One night around 3am, I was sitting on the sofa with my tiny baby sleeping in my arms, and I started to think about all the things I wanted and needed to hear. I thought about how comforting it would be to have the inner thoughts of another mother to help me through that challenging time. A full year later, the idea came to me again and, while all my feelings of being a new mother were still fresh enough in my mind, I sat down to write this book.

While not all my thoughts will be true for you, I hope some resonate and help you feel seen in this miraculous, vulnerable, raw and exciting time. And I hope you enjoy spending some time with me during this transformational point in your life.

Also, I'm about to say it a lot, but I need to say it here too -

You are doing a great job, well done, mom!

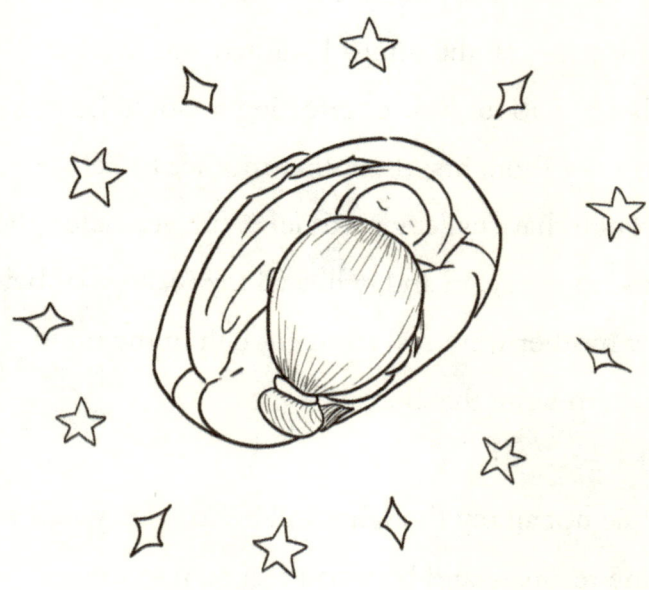

1. YOU JUST HAD A BABY!

This tiny creature was completely hidden away, you were sensing them through movements and feelings, a little like watching the shadow of a whale moving deep under water. And now they are right here in front of you and you can see their face and their eyes and touch their tiny fingers. You just had a baby, you did it!

However that baby came out, they are with you now (even if they are in the NICU, they are here, a huge part of your world and heart). They have the best mother for them, and they are so lucky. Take care of yourself, rest when you can, and know that however you had your baby, you did it! You just had your baby.

Well done, you're doing so great. You've been brave and strong, and now your baby is with you. Great job, mom.

2. YOU JUST BROUGHT YOUR BABY HOME FOR THE FIRST TIME

Congratulations, your baby's home! And you get to be home too, perhaps for the first time in a little while. How does it feel to be home with your baby? Whether everything is tidy and in place, or it's a mess and you still have nursery furniture left to build, you are a great mother. Babies don't need perfection - they just need milk, sleep, clean diapers and love.

It might feel a bit like being thrown into the wild west, suddenly being self-sufficient and expected to take care of this little life on your own. You have got this. If you feel afraid and you don't know all the answers, and you're scared of making mistakes, then you are like all the other new mothers in the world feeling exactly the same way. Like all the mothers who have ever existed in the world now and before us. A long and unbroken lineage of people feeling just the way you feel right now.

3. I'M SO TIRED, IS IT MEANT TO BE THIS HARD?

If you're tired, more tired than you've ever been in your life, like you've unlocked a new level of tired that you didn't know existed, then you are a mom. This is an incredibly hard part of the journey, and you are doing so well. It is hard. What you are going through is hard. And you are doing great. Whether you have help or not, whether you need to find help or not, you are doing a great job. This is probably the most tired you will ever be in your whole life, and when it's over, it will be behind you. But for now, just do what you can, the way you can do it. You are doing your best, you are doing so great, you are such a great mom.

It is exhausting, and it is love like you've never known, and it is tiring, and that love might not feel as strong if postpartum hormones and fatigue are clouding it over, but that's okay too, because it will be there, waiting for you. And getting help if you need it is okay too, it's more than okay. This is the most tired you're ever going to be in your life and you are surviving and being a great mom and I'm so proud of you. This will pass, you will sleep again, but for now you are doing the work and you are amazing. You are such a great mother in every way you show up for your child and show up for yourself. Even when you are exhausted and your hair is a mess and you can't remember when you last brushed your teeth, you are an incredible mother and person and your baby is lucky to have you.

4. HEALING FROM BIRTH

Wow! You gave birth. You are amazing! However it went, you did so great. Things often don't go according to plan, so if your birth experience didn't, you might be feeling raw emotionally. And if it did go to plan you might still be feeling a bit raw. You just had an experience a lot of people can't relate to and you're expected to be a good mother while healing from one of the biggest traumas the human body can go through. A miracle too, yes, but also a trauma. Take the care of yourself that you need to. You more than deserve it.

Your body produced life, sustained it, nurtured it and brought it into the world. It is amazing. *You* are amazing. Be gentle with yourself. Take time when you can. Find comfort in small rituals like showers and cups of tea and random moments of beauty like watching the light filtering through the trees.

If there is ever a time to take care of yourself, it is now. Be kind to yourself. Let standards slip if it means putting yourself first. Let the dishes be dirty, let the laundry pile up if you need to. Give yourself nurturing, nourishing moments of peace when you can. You deserve love, healing and support. And if you haven't already, just know that you *will* heal from the emotional and physical weight of pregnancy and birth. You will feel like yourself again. And until then, be tender with yourself, dear heart. Be exquisitely tender.

5. YOU ARE DOING AN AMAZING JOB!

It might not feel like it right now, but you are doing great. You really are. This part of motherhood is really hard, and you are doing it. You might be feeling like you have to do everything exactly right, clean every bottle perfectly, make the milk exactly the right temperature, track and time everything, and on top of that, try to keep the house in some kind of order. But while there are some things that are important to do right, others you can let slide. You are doing a lot right now and you're doing great. Even if you haven't seen the vacuum cleaner for a month.

You and your baby are on a journey that is going to last the rest of your life. And you may feel tired or overwhelmed at times, but you are strong and resourceful and intelligent and kind and you're a great mother. You are doing a great job, you really are. Well done, mom!

6. BABY, WHY ARE YOU CRYING?!

Has your baby ever just refused to stop crying no matter what you try? And you're rocking and shushing, doing bicycle kicks, offering milk, bicycle kicks, burping, bicycle kicks, soothing, swaying and bouncing like a sleep-deprived Tigger? Why has nature designed our babies to have only one tool of communication, and it's screaming in a way that stresses us out? Are new moms not already stressed enough? Did nature have to design the sound of our baby's cry to be one we hate the sound of, but we have to hold them close and it's right next to our ear and it feels overwhelming and never-ending?

And has it ever made you feel like you're a bad mother? When you're so far past your wits' end, that you feel like one nerve stretched taut, holding onto a screaming little life that is telling you you're doing everything wrong. Have you ever had to just put them down screaming for a bit and walk away, so that you can calm down long enough to become a person again? You are not alone. Those times when the baby won't stop crying are the most difficult, frantic-problem-solving, urgently-experimenting-with-different-techniques, pushing-through-overwhelm, hiding-our-frustration-and-maybe-embarrassment-if-we're-out-in-public, gritting-our-teeth-and-wanting-to-roll-on-the-floor-and-scream-ourselves, times we will ever go through.

I don't know what's worse - the thin reedy wahh, the pathetic wail or the urgent scream, or any of the hundreds of varieties of baby cry out there guaranteed to make us jump into alert-mom mode, our serenity left in the dust behind us. It can be as loud as a siren, but different, because at least sirens have a purpose. Sometimes our baby just seems to cry because they exist and there's nothing we can do. After cycling through all the things several times, sometimes we just have to give up and hold them. This tiny creature completely dominating us and our ear drums.

You are not alone in the stress, frustration, worry, embarrassment, feeling of failure. Every mom has been there. We all get it.

Keep breathing mom, you are doing a great job, even when it might not feel like it. Even when you have to put them down for a moment and step out for a cup of tea, scream into your pillow or take a long, slow breath. Especially then. You are being a great mom. Your baby *will* stop crying. You are going through a very hard part of the journey right now, but it's going to get better. So much better you might even forget all about how difficult this part was.

So keep going, you're doing great! And keep breathing mom!

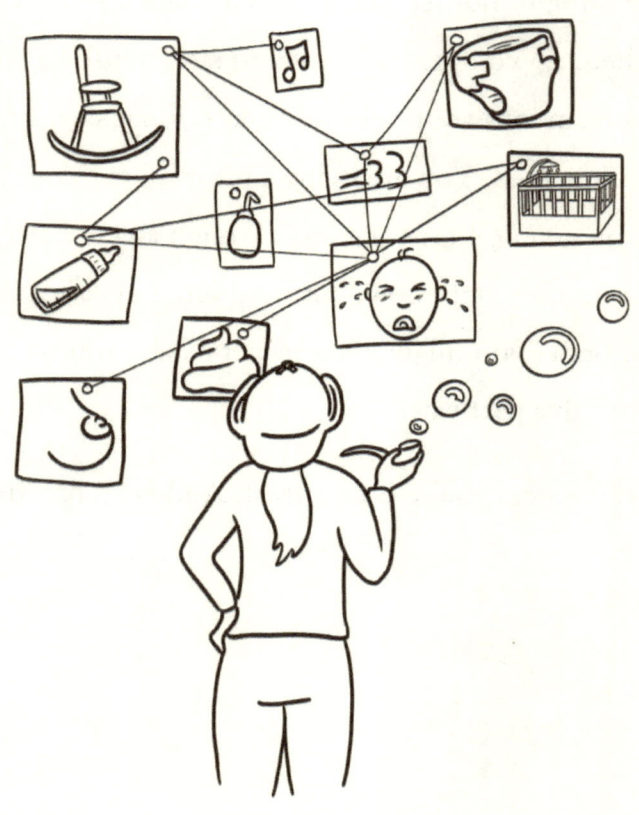

7. YOU'RE FIGURING THIS ALL OUT

If you find yourself blurry-eyed asking the internet what color poop is meant to be at 3 in the morning, trying to figure out why something as simple as putting a nipple in a mouth feels like trying to solve a Rubik's cube, wondering how to take care of a newborn and also have a poop when you need to poop, or have a shower and wash your hair, oh my goodness how good it feels to wash your hair, if you're flicking through baby books, and reaching out to people for advice, and asking the internet a million questions that make you seem obsessed with every substance a baby body can exude, then you are figuring this all out. And that is exactly what you are meant to do.

You are doing it, you are doing great, you are figuring this all out, and you are a great mom!

8. THE BLURRY-EYED MIDNIGHT MOTHER'S CLUB

You're staying up late more often than a college student right now. And I bet you've noticed something new, like when the sprinklers come on at night or how your street looks at 4:00 in the morning or maybe when the birds start singing. There's something special about inhabiting hours you never used to, like you're part of a secret club. And you are, you're now in the Midnight Mother's Club, the 1 a.m. internet-searchers, the awake-at-2a.m.-chat, the 3 a.m. TV watchers, the 4 a.m. blurry-eyed-social-media-scrollers, the 5 a.m. trying-not-to-fall-asleep-while-holding-the-baby-people, the 6am I-may-as-well-stay-up-now-posse.

If you're finding it hard to stay awake, then you are part of a huge group of blurry-eyed mothers. Also, if you're listening to me read this on the audiobook, I'm not sure my voice is going to be great at helping you stay awake (people tell me it's relaxing). But since you're with me, I just want to say that *you* are doing an incredible job. No matter what stains you have on your clothes right now (over-the-shoulder milk stains, anyone?), and no matter what kind of bird's nest you're rocking as a hairstyle, you are doing *so great*. And you are part of a members' club of nighttime parents all around the world watching TV, eating snacks over their baby, googling random questions and scrolling through social media, while everyone else sleeps. Welcome to the club, Midnight Mother!

9. YOU ARE AN AMAZING MOTHER

You are such an amazing mother, and you are doing so great, even when you think you're not, you really are. You're a wonderful mother, your baby or babies are so lucky to have you. Well done mom, good job mama!

You are a loving, gentle, wise, kind, intelligent, caring and nurturing mom. Whether you have a mother to tell you that or not, I am here to tell you that _you_ are a _great mother._ I know it, your baby knows it, and you know it too, even if that is quite deep down right now.

You are an amazing mother, even if you don't feel like one at the moment. Even if you're riding the dragon of postpartum emotions, that is okay. This experience is all a part of being an amazing mother. Getting help when you need it is also part of being an amazing mother. So, whatever this journey looks like for you, you are doing such a wonderful job and I am so proud of you. This is it. This is the work, and you are doing it. Great job, you amazing mom you!

10. RIDING THE EMOTIONAL DRAGON

Sometimes postpartum emotions are like riding a fire-breathing dragon. It doesn't care if society or social media wants you to be demure and such a tidy, kind and calm mother, like someone advertising a fabric softener. Sometimes you're going to want to scream, to be messy, to throw feelings around like bricks through windows. You might need to scream into a pillow, cry into a pillow, swear into a pillow. Your pillow might be doing some heavy lifting at the moment. You might need to talk to a friend or a partner or someone in your family or another mother or a professional.

Whatever you need right now, it is important to get it. Because you are not just a new mother, you are a new mother who is also riding a raging dragon. And that is really impressive, even if most other people can't see it. Other new moms can see it and they know you are a warrior. And whether you need to get help or not, you are a great mother, riding a fire-breathing dragon like a freaking superhero.

11. FEELING IRRITATED BY THE PEOPLE YOU LOVE

After you create the little person that you love so intensely, or will love intensely after the postpartum cloud has passed, you might be surprised to find yourself also getting very irritated with the people in your life that you love, including pets. It's normal. Someone's breathing weird or washing the bottles wrong or putting this there or putting that over here, and it's in the way, or it's in the wrong place, or it's just wrong, wrong, wrong. It's normal.

Try to be kind to yourself, you've just been through a lot. You haven't slept, your hormones are very much doing their own thing in a way that's not always going to be helpful to you, you've been through pregnancy and birth. So, if someone that you love is suddenly incredibly irritating, don't worry. It's most likely not a forever thing, it's just a part of this season. Take a deep breath, go for a walk, have a 5-minute rant into your journal or to your friends or both. The odds are very good that this feeling is going to pass in its own time. And that might be really annoying to hear when you're right in the middle of it. But although it is intense, it's not necessarily real. So take a deep breath, let it out, repeat. This is not the time to commit a murder. You are going to feel like yourself again. And the things that are irritating you are likely going to just fade away. And if they don't, you can go see a professional because they know all about it and can help.

In addition to seeing a professional, there's always chocolate. Even when you are as grumpy as fudge, you're doing great, mom.

12. SETTING YOUR BOUNDARIES

Some of us like to be alone with our new baby, others want a few people around, and some of us like a large family group. Whatever you need, whatever is good for your mental and physical health, is what you need to prioritize right now. But sometimes people take a new baby as an invitation. A baby is not an invitation. They are a tiny person who is completely dependent on you, takes up all of your time and stretches you to your limit. This is not a good time for you to need to host people, or cater to their emotions. This is the time for *you* to be taken care of by *others*. This is a time for you to feel safe within the fortified walls of your boundaries with whatever you need to heal emotionally, physically, psychologically, and spiritually. For you to have the space to transition into your new life as a mother, to bond with your baby and with your partner if you have one, and to figure out your new life together.

Other people may feel intense needs too, and that is very much their issue to deal with. The idea of strong boundaries might seem strange, especially to people from very social, living-all-together cultures. But I think it comes down to two main things: 1. who we are as people and what we need as a result and 2. the intentions of the people who want to visit. Of course, it would be lovely to be surrounded by people who want to take care of us as new mothers, but so many new moms are pushed aside by people who want to get to the baby. And the baby only wants and needs her parents. She has a very small, tender world. And new mothers need love and support to recover from the immense experience of pregnancy and childbirth and becoming a mother for the first time. So, it's a good time to be realistic about what you need, and honest in communicating that. If you need someone to come and clean your kitchen, not to hold the baby while *you* clean, tell them directly.

Your boundaries are like the walls of your castle and if you have to constantly tend to the walls, then you can't be present with your new baby or yourself, or rest and relax properly, which is essential for your recovery and to help you cope with the lack of sleep. So, being clear about your boundaries is very good for you and for your new family too. If you find that hard, it's not unusual. So many of us have been raised to put the needs of others first. Right now, *your* needs come first. They come first. You are important. You are a new mother, and you deserve support, love and respect. You deserve to feel safe within your castle with whoever you choose to invite into it, or not to. But it is your castle. No one can lower that drawbridge except you.

Here are some phrases that may help you to maintain your boundaries:

- no thank you
- not right now, thank you
- we don't need that right now, thank you
- we're not ready for that yet
- perhaps at a later date
- that won't work for us right now

- we are taking time to bond as a family
- thank you for supporting me and what I need as a new mother
- I appreciate you giving me the space I need
- we are looking forward to including you in the way that is right for our family
- I can't manage that right now
- I'm sure we can schedule some time in the future to do that
- please respect my needs as a new mother.

You are going through the biggest transition of your life, and you're likely to feel off-center and vulnerable. If there was ever a time to put your mental, emotional and physical needs first, it is now. You are extremely important and valuable. And to your baby, you are most of their world. Give yourself permission to create and maintain the space you need to heal and grow into this new phase of life with your baby. Great job, mom!

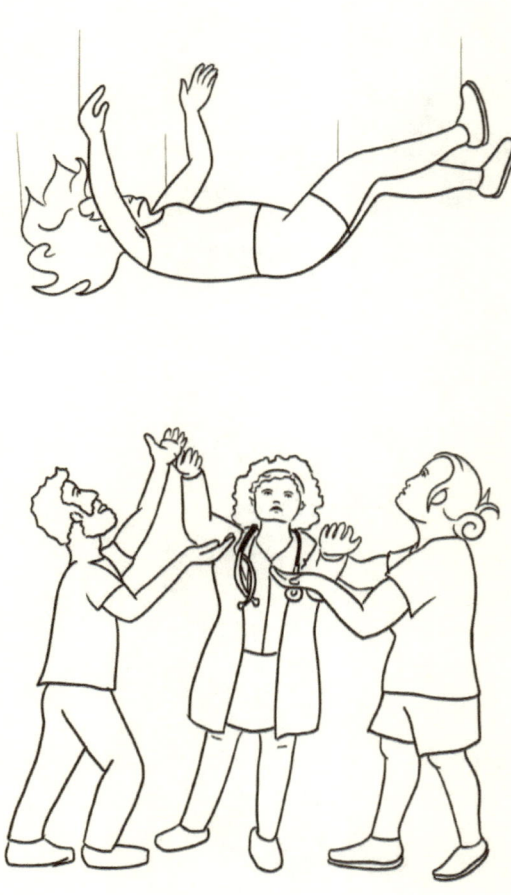

13. HOW LOW CAN YOU GO

There's sad, then there's blue, there's down, then there's depressed. And way below that is whatever emotional hell has been specially concocted for some new moms. Some of us get raging angry, like throwing things angry. Sometimes we get scared, of things that could happen, are maybe, absolutely happening right now, as if we are constantly teetering on the edge of a void. And sometimes we just feel like we toppled into that void and we're falling into darkness without end. Sometimes the low that we think is the lowest, gives way to a new way-down-low.

And it feels so real when you're in it. Like it's everything, and it's you and this is your life now. Like we'll never feel different from this. But it *isn't* true. This terrible feeling is temporary. It's a weird spell cast by hormones and sleep deprivation and being catapulted into a new life. But it's not real. I came through it myself, so I know how real it feels when you're in it and how it passes and you feel like you again. But even though it's going to pass – you absolutely do have to get help when you need it, and preferably before you need it.

There is a design flaw somewhere, when new, sleep-deprived moms have to take care of a new life, recover from pregnancy and birth, and also deal with some of the strongest emotions known to humanity. You are not meant to do it alone. These feelings are too big to keep to yourself. Talk to people, reach out to other mothers – many will understand, find a professional to talk to. Don't hold it all inside, it is too big. It can help to journal and find moments of joy and beauty that give you little lifts. But from my personal experience, there is no substitute for connecting with other people and working with sympathetic professionals.

Be gentle with yourself. This will pass, these real-feeling emotions are mirages in a postpartum desert and you will feel like yourself again. You are a wonderful person and mother, whatever you are feeling. <u>You</u> are a great mom.

14. YOU ARE A GREAT MOTHER

You are a great mother, so loving, so kind, intelligent, present, giving and thoughtful. Even if postpartum hormones have clouded things over temporarily so that you don't feel like a great mother, *you* are a wonderful mother. Sometimes you may feel like you're not doing enough or not performing somehow. But you are doing great. Your baby knows it, and I know it. You are a great mother whether you need to ask for help or not, whether you breastfeed or not. You show up every day for your baby and give them a way to enter into our world in safety, emerging little by little. Eyes opening, hands starting to explore, ears listening. You give them comfort, and through you, they start to know themselves. You are such a great mother. The way you comfort and hold your baby, respond to them, rock them, smile down at them, feed them. Every little thing you do is going into a big important bank of experiences that will help form the foundation of who they are. Whether you're home all the time, or you're doing daycare, whether it's mainly you, or you and a partner (or any other person helping out). You are a great mother.

You are so kind and attentive and giving. Your ready smile, your hand so fast to pat and soothe, your voice, your soft kisses and warm cuddles. You lay every part of yourself out for your baby so willingly, because you are generous with yourself. You deny them nothing. Even when you're stretched to your limit, you are a great mother. Even when you don't feel like it, you are a great mother. I hope you know that. But if you don't believe it yet, that's OK too. You will grow into believing it.

As with any new role it takes time to be fully comfortable in the scope and authority of it. In that case, please believe me, that soon you will fully know how much of a great mother you are. Until then, you will just have to take my word for it. Good job, mom!

15. BEING LET DOWN IN A WEIRD WAY

As a new mom, you might assume that everyone will show up for you in the way that you need. You *did* just have a baby, after all. But for many of us, at least one of the people or groups we're involved with will let us down in some way. For some of us it's well-meaning or not-so-well-meaning comments and advice, for others it's professionals that don't seem to care or who underperform. Many times it's something you don't expect that comes out of left field, like a friend telling you to hit the gym as soon as possible so you can bounce back, a stranger asking when the baby is due months after you've given birth, people overstepping because they want to be involved, other people seeming to care way too little, specialists telling you you're doing it wrong, someone you hire to help making you feel bad that you hired help. These are just a few of the strange things I've experienced and heard from my mom friends.

It doesn't make any sense that at the point you are at your most vulnerable and in need of support, some people will act out, or let you down in other ways. And the fact that it happens to so many of us is not great, but I hope that at least it makes you feel less alone. You are not wrong to feel upset. There is a saying to the effect that you forget the pain of childbirth, but you will never forget how people treated you. That is completely true. Before, during and after birth, you are very sensitive and open. If anyone hurts you at that time, you tend to remember it because it really stings.

So be kind to yourself. If any friendships you thought were solid start falling by the wayside, let yourself grieve. If you need to let people know what you need, or make different boundaries for a while, that's good too. You are going through a time in life where you are transforming into a new version of you. Like a butterfly in a chrysalis, you often can't handle the kind of stresses that might have just rolled off your back before.

So, be gentle with yourself. Prioritize the things that are working for you, move away from the things that are not. Find the professionals who are kind to you as well as competent. As much as possible, insulate yourself from unhelpful people and environments, while you take the time to evolve into this new, stronger version of yourself. You will be more than capable of dealing with negativity soon enough. But just for now, if you need to, give yourself permission to be exquisitely sensitive and to rest in the peaceful oasis you make for yourself.

You are important, so investing in your wellbeing is very smart. You deserve all the love and respect and to choose what to let into your space right now.

Take huge care of yourself precious lady.

16. YOU CLIMB A MOUNTAIN ONE STEP
AT A TIME

You climb a mountain one step at a time, and you carve a sculpture one chisel tap at a time. Don't focus on how the top of the mountain looks so far away, don't focus on how the sculpture just looks like a piece of rock. Everything you're doing now *matters*. Whether you are doing it well or just well enough, this is the work, it matters, and you're doing great. You're climbing the mountain one step at a time, one hug at a time, one night feed, one bottle, one pump, one internet search, one bath, one cup of tea, one coffee, one TV show, one meal, one bottle wash, one text to a friend, one photo, one breath, one moment of self-care. You're climbing this mountain, this is you doing it. It all matters. And *you* matter.

You're climbing this mountain, and one day you will look down at how far you've climbed, and you'll have a wonderful view as far as the eye can see. But for today, all you need to do is take one small step at a time, and that is far more than enough.

17. YOU MAY FEEL ALONE, BUT YOU'RE NOT ALONE

You might be feeling alone right now. It might feel like too much work to leave the house and meet up with friends. Or you might be finding it hard to be having such an intense experience that you can't articulate to people who aren't going through it too and who don't understand. And that gap in understanding might feel lonely. Or you might be feeling like you miss your old life and who you were, and you miss being that person and knowing her and being able to be her with your friends. Or you may be feeling a bit off, and disconnected from the world, out of the day-to-day running and happening of things, and that might make you feel lonely too. Or your postpartum hormones may be ganging up on you and telling you that you're more alone than you are. So, for whatever reason, you may be feeling very alone right now.

But you are *not* alone. You have people who love you and even more future friends coming your way. If you need to reach out and talk to your friends, do that. If you need to find new friends, do that too. Talk to your family, talk to the person bagging your groceries, talk to people. Reconnect. Becoming a mother and going through childbirth and all those feelings can really make some of us feel like we've moved to a different planet. But don't worry, your old self, your relationships, your connections, your place in the world, it's all still there. It's just going to be a little different, but different can be better too.

And as a new mom, you are definitely not alone in your experience, or how you feel. Today around 385,000 babies will be born. That's probably over 350,000 mothers at least, feeling exactly the way you're feeling right now. You're not alone. All other new mothers know exactly how you feel. There are around two billion mothers in the world in total, and now you are one of them. One of us. You are not alone. You are now a member of the new mothers' club. Welcome, you amazing mom, you.

18. THE CONTRADICTORY THOUGHTS OF MOTHERHOOD

- Your eyes are so beautiful, please don't open them! Please stay asleep a bit longer so I can regain a scrap of selfhood long enough to last my next shift as Mom.

- I want to show you to everyone so they can see how lovely you are, and I want to keep you all to myself, because you're so precious to me.

- You are so incredibly tiny and fragile-looking. I want you to grow up strong and resilient and eventually go out and take your place in the world. But I also want you to stay so small that you can fit snugly into my arms and I can remain a whole world of warmth around you.

- I need help, but I don't want to ask for it.

- Pictures of mothers are so gentle and endlessly patient, and the love I have for you is the tenderest thing, but sometimes I also really want to shout and throw things.

- I want to sleep, but I also need to shower. I want to shower, but I also need to sleep.

- I want to learn from the experience of other mothers and also do it all my own way.

- I want to find out what other people say is the best thing to do, and then I want to use my gut.

- My friends miss hanging out with the old me, so I guess she was pretty great, but I also need them to love and see the new me, like old me with a cool new annex built onto it.

- I don't want to be the person boring you by showing you photos of my baby. Also, look at all these photos of my baby.

- I love my partner and/ or pets and I am also very irritated by my partner and/or pets.

- I want to care what society thinks I should be at least a little bit, and I also want to be feral. Feral mother growls low when you give unsolicited advice. Grrrrrrr. Annoy her at your peril.

19. UNSOLICITED ADVICE SUPPOSITORY

Do you feel like you've just become some kind of lightning rod for unsolicited advice? You're not wrong.

There's something magical about a baby. They're like tiny magnets for interest and love, but also grabby hands, advice and judgment. As a mom you now face in-the-moment dilemmas where you have to immediately gauge if someone is nice/ nuts/ wise/ a dumb-dumb and if you'll have to quickly block people from grabbing at your baby's toes/ fingers/ chubchub rolls or cheeks.

It's a bit like being some kind of diplomat-warrior. Smiling, while also poised to parry an unsolicited piece of advice or wandering hand. Have you seen those zombie movies where they stumble around craving young flesh? It reminds me a bit of that. Most people are really nice, but some of them do love to randomly grab at your baby. Do they sanitize their hands first? No. Do they ask first? No. Because you might refuse, and they want what they want. I have experienced a ton of really nice interactions with people too, but I've also had to (try to) protect my baby from the grabby hands that come out of nowhere and it was worse while I was a newer mom. It sounds harsh, but it's like people can tell you haven't quite got your sea legs yet and they can still get away with shiz.

Sometimes when someone manages to cross a boundary in a way you didn't see coming, you might feel stunned afterwards, or worse, like you failed. You *didn't* fail, you just learned. There are weirdos out there, and some of them love babies. You did nothing wrong, other people need to grow the fudge up and respect you and the whole concept of personal space.

And the advice! Oh, the advice. Depending on your luck, around 10% of it will be helpful and 90% will make a mockery of common sense and medical advice. "My baby had toys with lead paint and it didn't do him any harm," "she's thirsty, give her some water" (don't do that!!!) "you need to… [insert stupid comment]."

Some people are lovely and genuinely want to help, while others seem lonely and just want to feel relevant or feel superior. The vulnerability of new motherhood can embolden some people to cross boundaries.

Big props to the people who help new moms when we need it. And to all the people who dole out unwanted criticism and advice, I recommend you take your own medicine and shove it up your a**, please and thank you. New moms have enough to deal with already.

You! You're being a great mom. I see you doing what you're doing. You are awesome.

20. SOCIAL MEDIA MONSTER MOTHER

Sometimes on social media you'll see moms who get up at 4am to run 8 miles, then simultaneously breastfeed, meal prep and drink a green juice. They have to be on drugs - there's no other explanation.

Moving for joy and to feel connected to our bodies is great, but there's no need to act like we're at bootcamp (unless that's something you actually benefit from). We are enough as we are; we don't need likes, or buns of steel and washboard abs, or to be "the best mom", which people have insanely high expectations of, by the way.

So, if social media is throwing up accounts of "perfect moms" and you're starting to feel icky, just close it. The machine of buy-something-you're-never-enough is not trying to make you feel good or like yourself. And life is too short to be comparing our real lives to the best-looking, scripted moments of others.

You know what's better than a "perfect mom"? A real mom. A sane mom, an interesting and happy mom. An imperfect mom. Someone you actually want to get to know, not someone who seems to run on fumes. Someone who's a bit messy round the edges. Someone who allows imperfections in themselves and others.

Who cares if your kitchen is a mess if your baby's getting cuddles and you're getting sleep and pets get the occasional scritch-scritch when you can manage it. You are a real person, you're not built for likes, you're built to live. *To live*. So, let's not be afraid to be real.

And also, *no one* wants to be friends with those people.

You are way more fun and cooler. Way, wayyyyyyy cooler.

21. NEW MOM HURDLES

You're going to face some hurdles as a new mom, like: your first walk outside with the baby, your first guests, your first doctor's visit, your first car/ train/ plane ride, your first night out, your first anything at all as a mom. It's normal to feel nervous about it.

The first solo trip outside of your "new baby bubble" can feel scary, even though you don't have to worry about looking after the baby at all. The outside world can feel so foreign, even though you've lived in it your whole life. Because now, in a sense, you are also brand new - you are emerging into it as a new mother. That might feel quite tender.

You can try breathing deeply, giving yourself comfort like wearing a soft sweater, ensuring you have the support you need, like meeting or texting a friend while you're out. To boost your confidence, why not think about some of your biggest past achievements and the challenges you've overcome. You are a strong and resourceful person.

Also remember: other moms go through these exact same feelings. They are <u>real</u>. And at the same time, you have got this. You've got it.

Go get 'em momma!

22. BUILDING YOUR SUPPORT TEAM

Just like a Formula One driver pulling into a pit stop, or a successful CEO with highly competent employees, we need support from other people to thrive and do a good job. While some of the messaging around motherhood wants us to believe mothers are saints (martyrs) who can cope on their own, that just isn't true. And why would that be desirable anyway? Why would we suddenly decide not to accept any help when embarking on one of the hardest and most important tasks of our lives? It wouldn't make any sense.

So, all moms need support, but it can look different for each of us. From the stalwart introvert who only needs one best friend, to the mom who loves a humming, vibrant community around her, there's no right or wrong answer here. And what we need now as a mother might be different to what we needed in the past. The social butterfly may want time to rest in a cocoon now, while the loner may suddenly want a village.

Whatever you need right now to support you in motherhood is valid. And it's even better if that support helps you to sustain your energy and a sense of who you are. I feel like the moms who have time to take pleasure in their passions or hobbies, and feel connected to themselves, have a much more fulfilling time postpartum. Help comes in many forms including: doctors, other moms, friends, cleaners, babysitters and more. What help do you need?

Motherhood is one of the most important jobs in society – we are raising an emotionally-intelligent, kind and resilient next generation. The future citizens of the world. That is quite an undertaking for you, so I hope you can give yourself permission to get whatever help that you need, and not downplay your needs or the effort you are putting in.

Finally, I just want to say that are a wonderful mother, whether you are surrounded by helpers or hoping for more. And also, that you deserve the support you need to be a wonderful mother who often has a smile on her face.

I know it doesn't always feel easy to reach out for help or connection. What helped me was realizing that other mothers were often feeling the same way as me, that specialists want to help us and that I mattered, even when my postpartum emotions didn't make me feel like I did.

And you matter too. You are doing a wonderful job, mom!!

23. WILL I EVER FEEL LIKE ME AGAIN?

You are a mother now, And. The And is everything you were before you stepped into this role. This role that sometimes feels so all-encompassing, all-important, perhaps even all you are allowed to be. Little or big bits of society may tell you that *Mother* is all you get to be now. Wrong. Wrongo! Wrong.

You are a mother And. You are a multi-layered, multi-faceted human being. An artist perhaps? An advocate, a lover, a creator, a businesswoman. An *interesting* person. You never stop being an interesting person. You are everything you were before, but now with a baby in the sidecar on the motorbike of your personality. It may not feel like it now, now that you've been getting your PhD in random facts about baby care and going through what might feel like the hazing phase of your parenthood journey.

It might not seem like you will ever feel like yourself again, but trust me, the old you is there waiting for you.

Wise. Knowing herself. She's lying in wait for the moment she gets to pounce on you with the desire to make something or go for a night out or simply wear something fancy. She's there, she'll always be there. The best friend, mother, guide, creative, the funny one, every single part of you that makes up you, as your own brilliant, spirited self. They're all waiting until you're ready, so they can merge with your new mother-self, like colors of paint pooling and mixing together to create an exciting new painting. You haven't lost yourself, even if you feel a little lost. You have gained a new part of yourself and soon every part of you will be hanging out together, having fun. Until then, you are still important. You are still interesting. You are a great mother And. You are still a really cool person. It is all still there, I promise. Great job, mom and fully rounded human being who is, and will always be, an important member of our society.

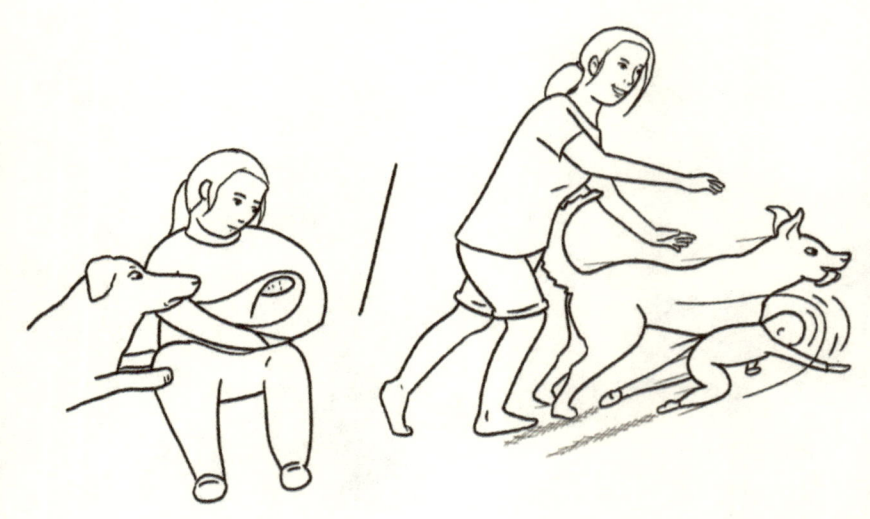

AFTERWORD

My baby's one now. She's a whole year old! I couldn't imagine that far ahead when she was a little potato in my arms. I could barely think forward to the next day, the next meal, or the next feed.

Looking back, it was such a raw time for me, healing from birth and pregnancy while being sleep deprived, while also feeling misunderstood by some people I knew, at the same time as feeling the most understood by people I didn't know at all. Strangers who gave me knowing looks in the street and encouraging smiles.

This short book of encouraging words and sketches has been my version of giving you a knowing look in the street, an encouraging smile, a "good job mama" in passing, to lift you up when you feel like crying into your sink full of baby bottles and/or pump parts. Crying in the shower. Crying anywhere, really. Or just feeling like you're unsure, or down, or lonely, or like you're grieving your old life, while being weirdly happy to have your baby at the same time.

Whatever you are going through, you are doing great. You are an amazing mom and your baby is so lucky to have you.

Thank you for spending this time with me! I hope you take good, luxurious care of yourself, love and invest in yourself and believe that you are a wonderful mom and human being, just like your little one(s) does. Take care and bye-bye for now!

Dear mom,

A big ask from me to you - if you think this book would benefit another mom, please leave a review wherever you buy or find books, or share it with friends.

It helps me so much, because the more readers like you spread the word, the more time I can spend writing and hopefully helping people.

Thank you so much! I really appreciate your support. And I hope you're doing great,

Suzanne x

SUZANNE'S OTHER BOOKS

FEELING HAPPY, FEELING STRONG

An easy-to-read guide to working through your stress and anxiety.

Learn how to connect with your body, change your physical state to change your feelings, work with your emotions, forgive yourself for being imperfect, self-reflect and relax.

This accessible book has simple yet effective tips and exercises you can put into practice right away. Get your copy to start releasing your stress and anxiety today!

PERFECT: A SELF-LOVE ADVENTURE

An inclusive picture book that teaches kids self-love. The children you'll meet in this book are Black, White, Asian, South American and Native American. Some of what makes them special includes a limb difference, using a wheelchair, a port-wine stain, visual impairment and a cleft lip and palate.

However, Perfect is not about differences and disabilities, it is all about acceptance, resilience and self-love.

The characters love and accept their unique bodies, enjoy movement, know they are perfect, accept difficult situations, work through emotions and know that love is there whenever and wherever they need it. Your child will love spending time with them.

MOVING STRETCH: WORK YOUR FASCIA TO FREE YOUR BODY

This accessible guide to stretching can help you change your body in only 10-20 minutes a day!

It includes:
• An introduction to stretching, the fascia, and flexibility
• Easy-to-follow guidance on how to stretch for maximum impact
• Effective stretches and warm-ups for the whole body
• Goal-oriented stretch routines for: flexibility, hip mobility, posture, unhunching and more!
Get this bestseller today to start feeling fit and strong in your body.

OTHER RESOURCES AVAILABLE

For a wide range of self-help resources check out www.suzannewylde.com. You will also find helpful tips on my Instagram @suzanne_wylde.

Thank you for reading all the way to the end! Take care of yourself and see you next time!